Soulful Reflections

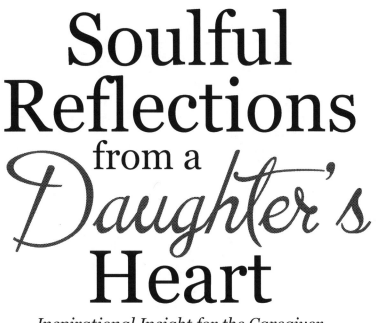

from a

Heart

*Inspirational Insight for the Caregiver
of a Loved One with Dementia*

JAN BLAKELY

WESTBOW
PRESS®
A DIVISION OF THOMAS NELSON
& ZONDERVAN

Scripture taken from the New King James Version. Copyright © 1979, 1980, 1982 by Thomas Nelson, Inc. Used by permission. All rights reserved.

Patty Cochran, The Fly, personal journal entry, 2016. Used by permission.

WestBow Press books may be ordered through booksellers or by contacting:

WestBow Press
A Division of Thomas Nelson & Zondervan
1663 Liberty Drive
Bloomington, IN 47403
www.westbowpress.com
1 (866) 928-1240

ISBN: 978-1-5127-5576-3 (sc)
ISBN: 978-1-5127-5577-0 (hc)
ISBN: 978-1-5127-5575-6 (e)

Library of Congress Control Number: 2016915003

Print information available on the last page.

WestBow Press rev. date: 9/12/2016

This is dedicated to my beloved mother, Patty Cochran. She was the epitome of a strong woman and the best role model a daughter could ever ask for. She truly was the woman described in Proverbs chapter 31.

I want to thank my family and friends for their support and encouragement.

I would like to acknowledge Dr. Peggy Noel and the staff at Memory Care for the wonderful care that they provided to my mother and my family as we dealt with my mother's dementia.

Contents

Introduction

My mother suffered from a type of dementia. In addition to being the daughter of someone with this terrible disease, I was also her caregiver. It is a role that nothing can prepare you for and definitely calls for on-the-job training. There are books to help explain the disease process. There are support groups to help you through it, that is if you can break away to attend. Most of the time, I just had to rely on my faith to get me through.

Being a follower of Christ, I began searching for a devotional book that was specific for the caregiver of a family member with dementia. I did not find anything that met my need. I had been keeping a journal of the journey. So I decided to take some of what was in my journal and start writing my own devotional. One day I was writing in my notebook while traveling with my husband. Since he was a captive audience, my husband asked me to share some of what I had written. He was very touched by my entries, as his mother also suffers from severe dementia. He encouraged me to share it; he felt it could benefit others who are in the same situation.

My mother has graduated on to heaven since I first began this project. She was an artistically creative person in many ways. She loved to write stories and poems and continued to do so during her early years of dementia. So I share my heart with you as a way to honor my mother; I hope it will provide comfort and encouragement as you go on this journey of being a caregiver to a loved one who suffers with dementia.

"What a beautiful testimony to your mother's life, caregiving, and the power of faith to help one through the journey." - Margaret A. Noel, MD, Founder, Director Emerita MemoryCare

Chapter

1

Taking Care of Business

We began to notice subtle changes in Mom's behavior and in her capacity to remember things. She would frequently misplace things or put them away and not remember where she had put them. She was becoming more repetitive in conversation. We discussed these subtleties with a doctor. He did a few simple cognitive tests, which she passed. So he wrote it off to the aging process. Being her daughter, I was around her daily and more in tune with my mom than her doctor—who only saw her for a few minutes occasionally. So I was persistent about a more thorough workup. He made a referral to a gerontologist, which is a doctor who specializes in memory care. That was a godsend.

Mom went through a battery of tests that included an MRI of her brain. All family members were included in the interview process. As a result, we got the diagnosis of early onset dementia/cognitive impairment. Even though I suspected it, receiving the diagnosis was a blow. The doctor outlined what we could expect to happen over the coming years, but she was unable to provide defined times since we caught it early.

One important thing we knew we needed to do immediately, while Mom was still capable of managing her own affairs, was to get some critical documents in place. We needed to get her last will and testament updated, and we needed a general power of attorney and health-care power of attorney in place. Having these documents in place is biblical. Hebrews 9:16–17 says, "For where there is a testament, there must also of necessity be the death of the testator. For a testament is of force after men are dead, since it has no power at all while the testator lives." Having a will in place helps ensure that a person's wishes are known and carried out after death. It also helps the family avoid unnecessary state and court involvement. The power of attorney allows your loved one to choose his or her own representative to make business and healthcare decisions rather than having someone assigned who might not necessarily have the loved one's best interests at heart.

So let me encourage you. Everyone should make sure to have a will and a power of attorney in place. You never know when it might be needed. But in the case of when a loved one is diagnosed with dementia or cognitive impairment, these documents need to be in place as soon as possible—while the person is still competent and able to express his or her wishes.

Chapter

2

What Is a Legacy?

Ecclesiastes 7:1 says, "A good name is better than precious ointment; and the day of death than the day of one's birth."

My mom had always been so active both physically and mentally. She loved to read. She wrote short stories and poetry. Some of her poems were published. She loved to write a poem or story for a particular person and give it to them as a gift of the heart. She painted landscapes. She was a talented musician, playing the piano and accordion. The talent was in the fact that she played by ear and could not read music. She sang with a female version of a barber shop quartet called the Sweet Adelines. She was a substitute school teacher and child care provider. She was an avid gardener.

She was involved in many volunteer organizations helping others. For her involvement with the Red Cross assisting with disaster relief work, she was nominated and selected to be a local torch bearer for the 1996 Summer Olympics. The greatest thing that she ever did was to share the love of Christ with others, be it in word or deed. She made sure that her children were raised in the love and admonition of the Lord. I am a follower of Christ because of the witness of my mother.

In many cultures the greatest ambition is to have a reputation that is an honorable memory to the person's posterity. You can see examples of this daily when you read someone's obituary. It describes the legacy of that person to others unknown to the deceased. It also describes honored memories of that person to those who knew and loved the deceased.

If a person's life is such that what is left behind is a good name and reputation, then the day of death is simply an accounting of that life. You hope that it will be a victorious accounting of that life. The day of birth is the beginning of life, which is a clean slate. So to leave a lasting, positive legacy makes the day of death better than the day of birth. My mom touched so many lives in a powerful way. She truly left a great legacy.

Chapter

3

Heal Me

When Mom was first diagnosed with dementia, she was very angry about it. Many times she would become enraged and refuse to go to her memory care appointments. We would resort to all kinds of distractions to get her there. Several times she would refuse to get out of the car when we arrived at the office. But once we got her inside, she was as different as night and day. She would become so jovial and friendly, not at all like the person in the car.

There were many times we cried out to God for healing for Mom. He heard our cries and prayers, but it was not part of His master plan to provide healing. How could the God who spoke the universe into existence allow such a horrible disease to come upon my mother and then refuse to heal her? As followers of Christ, we must accept that even though we do not understand what God does, He knows what is best for us. I am not saying it is easy, but by faith I strive to accept it. I can only hold on to the promise of what is stored up for Mom in heaven for eternity.

We are to ask God for healing, as it says in Jeremiah 17:14: "Heal me O Lord and I shall be healed. Save me and I shall be saved; for You are my praise." But sometimes that healing will not be provided during our time on the earth. My mom was a follower of Christ and had been saved from the grips of eternal death. So, in essence, she was healed. She was spared eternal death and given eternal life in glory where there is no pain or suffering. When she crossed over from this life on the earth to eternity in heaven, she was healed in an instant, and she received blessings beyond imagination. That is the source of our hope during this time of suffering on the earth.

Chapter

4

Denial Is Not a River in Egypt

N o, denial is not a river in Egypt. That would be the Nile. But denial is considered to be the first stage of the grieving process. It is very hard to accept a life-changing diagnosis for a loved one, especially when the outcome will be one that steals away the existence of that person. This is typically associated with a diagnosis of cancer. But it is just as real with a diagnosis of dementia. The worst part of dementia is that your loved one is no longer there mentally or emotionally, but he or she is still there physically. That is why it is easy to say this is one of those conditions that are worse than death itself.

As a family member, you can remain in the state of denial far longer when dementia is involved. You play

Jan Blakely

it off and cover it up with excuses, trying to make it seem as though the dementia is nonexistent. You hide it from friends and all but the closest family members. If you don't talk about it or even say the word *dementia* out loud, it's possibly not true. You dare not say the word *dementia* to your loved one for fear of how he or she will react. He or she might become very angry at the mere insinuation of having memory issues. But the whole time you are in the state of denial, you are depriving yourself and your loved one of much-needed help in the early stages—help that can ease the transition to the later stages. By then, the adjustment is hard on everyone involved.

Denial is a form of bitterness. It can eat away at you. God's Word can be healing to the bitter spirit. Reading it can help give direction to joy and peace. Ephesians 4:31–32 says, "Let all bitterness, wrath, anger, clamor and evil speaking be put away from you with all malice. And be kind to one another, tenderhearted, forgiving one another, even as God in Christ forgave you."

Once you move past the bitterness wrought from denial, you are able to find strength to cope. As you are better able to cope, you are better able to care for your loved one with understanding, kindness, and compassion.

Chapter

5

I Am So Mad I Could Just ...

Anger is the second stage of the grieving process. It follows closely on the heels of denial (bitterness). Most times the anger is directed at God. How could He let it happen if He really loved us? Sometimes the anger gets directed at the person who is sick or dying. It is as if he or she intentionally got sick just to make you mad. Sometimes the anger can be turned on innocent bystanders. But it is most destructive when it is turned inward.

Anger can be very destructive if it isn't dealt with in the proper way. It has a way of festering and destroying you from the inside. You lash out at others inappropriately and say hurtful things. Like the toothpaste that has been squeezed out of the tube, words spoken in anger can never be taken back. Relationships can be damaged by words spoken in anger. The anger may be acted out directly, or it might be a product of inaction. When you realize that in your moment of anger you have physically or emotionally hurt the one person you are committed to caring for, you are overcome with guilt. Then you get mad for being mad. What a vicious cycle!

Sometimes I would get angry with my mom over the stupidest thing. It wasn't that I was angry with her, but the anger I was holding inside because of her condition would come spewing out at the worst time. She would look at me like a little lost puppy. Then I would feel all sorts of guilt and remorse. I would beat myself up over it for hours. But she would have forgotten about it seconds after it happened.

Psalm 37:8 says, "Cease from anger, and forsake wrath; do not fret – it only causes harm." There is a time and place for anger. Remember that Jesus had a righteous anger as He drove out the moneychangers and thieves from the temple. The Bible also tells us in Ephesians 4:26, "Be angry and do not sin."

So it is okay to be angry. God understands that emotion. Just make sure to understand your anger and deal with it appropriately. Then move on from it, and don't let it destroy you.

Chapter

6

Depression Is No
Laughing Matter

"Therefore the king said to me 'Why is your face sad, since you are not sick? This is nothing but sorrow of the heart'" (Nehemiah 2:2). Even though this verse was written hundreds of years ago, he could have been writing it directly to me today. The pain, sadness, and frustration you feel in your heart show in your outward appearance. It is true that heartache crushes the spirit.

Depression is the third stage of grief. Even though it is considered to be the third stage, you do not always go through the stages sequentially. You might skip one or even waffle back and forth between stages.

People who have not experienced grief firsthand can easily say, "Oh, just laugh it off and move on." That is easier said than done. Recognizing depression is vital to being able to overcome it, as opposed to it overcoming you. It is helpful to have someone to talk to. Fortunately, I have a very supportive husband. He listens to me as I pour out my heart through words and tears. Many times that is all he knows to do. But he fails to see that it might be all that is needed. When you are in the midst of depression, it can be hard for you to recognize when you need more than a sympathetic ear to help you get through it.

I rely on my faith to help get me through each day, especially the days that are heavy with sadness or frustration. I cling to Nehemiah 8:10: "For the joy of the Lord is your strength." But there are times when you need more. That does not mean that your faith is weak. God gave humans knowledge. From that knowledge we have physicians to help treat physical and mental illnesses. From that knowledge medications have been developed to treat physical and mental issues. Feeling the depression is a normal part of the process. But recognize and seek help when the depression starts to consume you. You cannot be there to care for your loved one if you are not taking care of yourself first.

Let's Make a Deal

F ar too often, when a loved one is seriously ill, people will start pleading and trying to make a deal with God to spare the pain and suffering of the loved one. Bargaining is the fourth stage of the grief process. The bargain could range from giving something up to stopping a behavior to starting a new behavior. Most often it is a deal in which the person will start going to church or turn his or her life around; in other words, the person gets right with God.

God very well may take you up on the bargain, so you need to be careful about the terms you negotiate. In the heat of emotion it is easy to make foolish promises to God. They may sound good at the time but not so good when you have to keep up your end.

God wants your obedience today and not promises for the future.

As my mother's physical state started to decline, I became more involved in her daily care. One day I felt a cold coming on. I asked God to spare me from getting sick. I needed to be at 100 percent so I could take care of Mom. I should have stopped there with my request. Rather, I added that He could bring any illness upon me after my mother passed if He would just let me stay healthy enough to care for her through her last days. Well, I did not get sick. I was feeling 100 percent healthy by the next morning.

In Judges 11:30–40 Jephthah made a hasty bargain with God. He promised to offer up as a burnt offering the first thing that came through his door as long as God delivered the Ammonites to him in battle. Little did he know that his daughter would be the first one through the door. Heartbroken, he explained to his daughter his hasty vow to God. She knew the importance of obedience and keeping a vow made to God. So Jephthah kept his end of the bargain, just as God had done.

I don't know what God will have in store for me as part of my bargaining request. But hopefully I will avoid casual and irresponsible commitments to God in the future and just strive for daily obedience. The lesson I learned was not to make hasty vows.

Chapter

Acceptance

The final stage of the grief process is acceptance. At this point you can really deal with what has happened. For some this can be a long road and a long time coming. Others get to this point quickly, saying, "It is what it is" and move on. Accepting it, however, does not necessarily make it any easier. It just gives a different perspective on the outcome. You are able to enjoy every minute of time spent with your loved one. You don't let the little things consume you. You can see the forest *and* the trees. Having faith in something better than this life gives you hope. When your loved one shares that same belief, the hope of a reunion in heaven is a promise; it is a reality realized when you have both passed on. Our faith is in a risen Savior. Through our faith we also will have eternal life in heaven.

At the point of acceptance you find peace and can rest. It does not mean that the road will be a bed of roses. There will be bumps all along the way. But once you have accepted what is going on, you will see that the bumps in the road are still part of the road and not something separate. Psalm 37:5–7 says, "Commit your way to the Lord, trust also in Him and He shall bring it to pass. He shall bring forth your righteousness as the light and your judgment as the noonday. Rest in the Lord, and wait patiently for Him."

Acceptance does not come easily. One day you may be okay with what has happened, and the next day you're not. It is an ongoing process. Acceptance comes when you recognize the situation without trying to change it. The protests cease. You come to a place where you can find peace and rest in the circumstance.

Chapter

9

Peace, Despite Our Trials

Being a caregiver can bring times of joy but also many hard times. It can be very trying when the person you dearly love is combative and resistant to everything you are trying to do to care for her or him. For example, she does not want to eat, so she throws the food on the floor or even in your face. She does not want to take a bath, so she hits you. She does not want to take the medicine, so it is inconspicuously tucked inside the cheek until it can be discreetly spit out and thrown away or even spit back at you. Maybe she has used a permanent marker, lipstick, or nail polish to color her eyebrows. You know this behavior is not in the nature of your loved one. She would be appalled at her actions if she was in her right mind. You also know you are doing the best you can, but these episodes can really wear you down physically, emotionally, and spiritually.

I have found that singing hymns or even reading scripture can soothe my mom at times when she is in one of those states. But even if it doesn't bring her a sense of calm, it brings me a sense of calm. I know that God loves her far more than I do, and I love my mom dearly. Sometimes the storms and trials may just be what I need to get me to slow down long enough to go to the source of true peace.

Romans 5:1–2 says, "Therefore being justified by faith, we have peace with God, through our Lord Jesus Christ through whom also we have access by faith into this grace in which we stand, and rejoice in the hope of the glory of God."

There are days that are beyond difficult as a caregiver. But when you look back, you realize that you were sustained by the grace of God. You know that the ordeal will eventually come to an end. So you just do the best you can while you still have the chance. Your reward will be realized on the other side.

Chapter

10

Not Just a Job

I am a nurse by profession, a daughter by birth, and caregiver for a loved one by destiny. Nurses usually provide care to heal. There are fields of nursing, however, that provide comfort and compassion to someone in the last days of life—hospice care.

As a nurse, I sought out any available cures for my mom's dementia. After all, she is my mother, and I needed her to be healed so that she could be with me for many days to come. I knew about every medication that had been prescribed. I researched all possible activities to keep her engaged and her mind from deteriorating. I had to stay in nurse mode because daughter mode could not handle watching the decline of my mother's physical and mental health.

I maintained a job outside the home, providing nursing care to others. This work was an outlet of sorts for me. I would come home in the evening and spend time doing what needed to be done for my mom. Sometimes it was just spending quality time with her. Then that day came that I needed to be with her throughout the day, being a more involved caregiver. My days and evenings were consumed with caring for her. As I watched her decline and grow closer to death, I just wanted to be the daughter and not the nurse. So hospice was initiated. Then I could focus on the daily minutia of care while the other healthcare professional could focus on the medical aspects of care.

There were times it was hard not to be the nurse. When I observed a change in Mom, I would note it and report it to the nurse. She would frequently remind me that those signs and changes were part of the process. She frequently gave me encouragement to just be the daughter.

Until you have walked in those shoes, no one can tell you the internal struggle and the stress you encounter as a healthcare professional when you are caring for a loved one for whom there is no cure. Their only relief comes with death. I have my calling as a nurse and a preferred field of nursing that aims at cures.

The hospice nurse is called in to a field of care and support for the dying. We are in the same field yet see a different outcome for our patients. But we do what we do the best way we know how for those who need us. Verse 5 in the third book of John says, "Beloved, you do faithfully whatever you do for the brethren and for strangers." So as I cared for my mother, I was taking care of family. The hospice nurse was caring for the stranger. But we did the best we could at all times.

Chapter

11

No Directory Assistance Required

In today's culture it seems that everyone has a cell phone. Just look around, and my point will be validated. They are talking, texting, posting, tweeting or sending some other form of communication to another person. Most people have no reservation about giving out their digits (today's lingo for phone number) to someone. No more writing it on your hand or on a check deposit slip because you can't find a piece of paper. You just tap the numbers in your phone, click save, and it's done. Your contact list just expanded.

When telephones first came out, not everyone had a phone. If you had a phone, you might be on a party line instead of having your own personal line. Phone numbers were very different. Instead of seven to ten digits, it was alphanumeric, such as BR549. But there is a phone number that just might be missing from a lot of phones or contact lists. And it could very well be the most important contact you could ever have: God. Yes, God has a phone number. It is an alphanumeric number. God's phone number is Jeremiah 33:3: "Call to me, and I will answer you, and will show you great and mighty things which you do not know."

Yes, God would love to have us call Him. He wants us to tell Him everything. He can be the best "bestie" if we allow Him. He desires for us to share our hearts with Him. Fortunately, we do not have to use any technology to call God. We just call His name and start speaking from our hearts. God will listen.

This is one number that I call many times a day. Talking with God is what has gotten me through this tumultuous journey with my mother. I have Him on speed dial. When caring for someone with dementia, there isn't a single day without some sort of challenge. Having someone to talk to when it gets bad really helps. Having God to talk to at a moment's notice is the best call you can make. I recommend that everyone keep God's phone number in their contact lists and call Him often.

Chapter
12

Growing Old with Dignity and Grace

" For by me your days will be multiplied and years of life added to you" (Proverbs 9:11). The senior years are referred to as the golden years of life. As you live through many life experiences you learn many lessons. Those life lessons are the source of wisdom that continues to guide you in your choices. The pundits always have the right food, best activity, and best life philosophy to enrich your life and add years to it. But their advice changes with the wind.

Everyone desires to grow old with dignity and grace. That's more the result of how you treat people and desire to be treated than any diet or activity. Maintaining dignity and grace is hard for those with dementia.

Instead of self-toileting, they are wearing diapers. Instead of self-grooming, they require a degree of assistance to shower, dress, brush teeth, and so forth. Rather than having the freedom to choose when they can perform their activities, they are required to abide by the schedule of the caregiver. It is important to allow them to have some input on the decisions about their care. Give them choices as to what to wear for the day, even though you will be dressing them. Allow them some say as to the timing of their baths; just don't let them derail you totally from bathing.

I made sure that my mom's hair was washed and curled a couple of times a week. I put a little makeup on her, even if it was just lipstick so that when she looked in the mirror she would see the beautiful person she was. Even though she was just going to spend her day sitting in the house, she had the sense that her appearance was up to her standards.

When you are performing the activities of daily living for your loved one, do so with the utmost respect and dignity. When your loved one has dementia, dignity comes from how the caregiver provides care rather than from anything he or she can do individually. Allowing your patient any possible personal input might be the only bit of control he or she has left. No one enjoys a life over which there is no control. Be the advocate to ensure that everyone who has contact with or is providing some degree of care for your loved one treats him or her respectfully. Be bold and step in when someone deviates from that standard.

They say what goes around comes around. One day you will be the older person who might need care. You will want to be treated with respect. Therefore, sow the seeds of dignity and grace when caring for others so that you will be able to reap the harvest when the time comes.

Chapter

13

A Time to Mourn

There are many reasons to mourn. But mourning is most often associated with death. Living with dementia of any type causes you to mourn the life of your loved one more than once. First you mourn the loss of that person while he or she is living because it gets to a point that the person becomes just a shell of who he or she once was. You do not have that person with you any longer.

Personality, memories, and engagement in life are gone. The physical body is there, but everything else is lost. So it is as if you mourn the loss on a daily basis. This grief can really take an emotional toll. It is a blessing, a big relief, when the physical death finally comes. You mourn for your loved one, but you can now see an end to the mourning period. Sure, you will miss the daily contact. But the person you know and loved was gone a long time ago.

Ecclesiastes 3:1–4 says, "To everything there is a season, a time to every purpose under heaven. A time to be born, and a time to die; a time to plant and a time to pluck up that which is planted; a time to kill and a time to heal; a time to break down and a time to build up; a time to weep and a time to laugh; a time to mourn and a time to dance."

This sums up the full gamut of emotions you feel as a caregiver. Maybe one day there will be healing for dementia. But until that time comes, you will definitely cry, laugh, and mourn as you care for your loved one. We have to discover, accept, and appreciate God's perfect timing through it all. Then that time will come, and we can repeat what King David said: "You have turned my mourning into dancing; you have put off my sackcloth and clothed me with gladness" (Psalm 30:11).

Now that my mother has passed on, I still mourn. I lost my mother a long time ago, when she was diagnosed with dementia. Only this time, my mourning is because of her physical absence. But I can celebrate the fact that her dementia is no more. She is now enjoying a glorified body in the presence of God.

Chapter

14

More Than Enough

When you are focusing a lot of your physical, mental, and emotional energy on caring for your loved one, you tend to lose yourself. You forget that you also need to take care of yourself. But your body will eventually give you clues or reminders. It might start off with occasional insomnia, which may progress to daily insomnia. You might grind your teeth so badly in your sleep that you develop pain in your jaw due to the stressed nerves surrounding your teeth. Your teeth may crack or become loose and fillings may fall out. Your digestive system may no longer work properly. You might get reflux with every meal or even without food. You may experience nausea, vomiting, or diarrhea that alternates with constipation. You might feel tired all the time. You may have moods that range

Jan Blakely

from happy to depressed and feel that your body is falling apart.

You tell yourself that you just can't take anymore. Just one more upset will put you over the edge. Then it happens—that one more thing. Someone else gets sick, financial hardships strike, or a loved one passes away. It could be anything. You know that you have reached your breaking point. You can't look anywhere but up when you are sitting on the bottom.

We should not have to wait until we are at rock bottom to look up. God is waiting for us to cry out to Him all along the journey. He is more than able to carry us through our storms. Second Corinthians 12:9 says, "And he said to me, 'My grace is sufficient for you, for My strength is made perfect in weakness.' Therefore most gladly I will boast in my infirmities, that the power of Christ may rest upon me."

It is in our weakness that we truly sense God's strength. We just need to stay connected to the power source. So when you think you have had more than enough, remember that God is more than enough to get you through.

Chapter
15

How Much More?

There is one question I have learned not to ask: How much more can I take? It seems that as soon as I ask it, that "more" happens. But it is not so much about how much we can or can't handle. It is about trusting God. He knows what our limits are. He tells us that we are not given more than we can handle. First Corinthians 10:13 says, "But God is faithful, who will not allow you to be tempted beyond what you are able, but with temptation will also make the way of escape, that you may be able to bear it."

If we belong to God, He will not allow any difficulty to come into our lives that we are not capable of bearing. Our strength to endure comes from God. Life is not easy. It is encouraging to know that we can face the difficulties with confidence in God's power and promise to overcome. There is a saying: "God doesn't give us what we can handle. God helps us handle what we are given." So when I cry out, asking how much more I can take, I just need to trust that God will get me through what He has brought me to.

As my mom continued to decline, the demands on me increased. It takes a lot out of you when you must do everything to just meet daily basic needs: feeding, grooming, dressing, and toileting. When someone has dementia, there are twists and turns daily. While cleaning up a mess in one room, she could slip out the door because she has figured out the new locks, and she could be gone in seconds. You could get her back in the house only to discover she has undressed and thrown part of her clothes in the trash. While getting her dressed again, you may notice she is chewing on something. You find that it is the pills you thought she had swallowed a few minutes before. You pray for her to take a nap just so you can have a few moments to quietly rest yourself. You just don't think you can go on. That is when you cling to the promise from Isaiah 40:31: "But those who wait on the Lord shall renew their strength; they shall mount up with wings like eagles; they shall run and not be weary; they shall walk and not faint." I only make it through each day because I know God knows the limits of what I can handle and gives me the strength to make it through.

Chapter
16

Patience, My Child

Patience may be a virtue, but it is not my forte. My husband frequently reminds me that I can be the most impatient person he has ever met. I admit that I have occasionally timed the waitress to see how long it takes her to come to our table once we have been seated. I have no qualms in verbalizing frustration when in line, and the person ahead of me is taking longer than I expect.

Part of this is my nature. Part of it is learned behavior. I spent most of my nursing career taking care of critically ill patients. So many times the situation called for quick action with an equally quick response. When you are caring for someone with dementia, patience takes on a whole new meaning. You have to be patient. The person in your care is trying to tell you something. The words come out jumbled or all confused, or maybe it even takes a while for them to come out. You may or may not be able to understand what's said. Simple tasks—eating, dressing, and bathing—can take longer because they are now more difficult to perform. It is really easy to throw up your hands and say, "Oh, just let me do it for you." But that benefits no one. Sure, it gets the activity done quickly. But your lack of patience has only created frustration for you both and can be demeaning to your loved one.

All those tricks you tried when raising children to help you keep your calm will come in handy once again. Step back, take a deep breath, and let it go.

God gives us many pointers on patience. Psalm 27:14 says, "Wait on the Lord, be of good courage and he shall strengthen your heart. Wait, I say, on the Lord." How much clearer can the message be? Patience will help us do what needs to be done. It will also bring strength of body and character and provide encouragement to both you and your loved one.

Chapter

17

Frustrated Beyond Belief

There are days when nothing goes right. You feel like beating your head against the wall because you are so frustrated with your loved one. You put clothes on that come off right away. Under the chair you find pills hidden that you believed were swallowed. You try to clean up after a bowel movement, only to spend more effort to stop him or her from handling it and getting it everywhere. You feel like a figurative firefighter, spending all your time putting out fires your loved one has started. You have no idea where you are going to get the strength to make it through the day. This is cyclic—day in and day out. Of course, some days are better than others. But the frustration remains.

Jan Blakely

Little do we recognize that our loved ones may well be equally frustrated. They are no longer the vivacious, independent, and strong people they once were. They must now depend on others to do almost everything for them. Decisions are made for them. I am sure my mom felt that she was no longer making a contribution but was a burden instead. Given the strong woman she once was, I can only imagine the frustration she felt but was unable to communicate. She would attempt to do something. Whatever it was she was doing made no sense to me. But I am sure that, in her mind, it made perfect sense. So I would try to organize or clean up the mess. And it went that way all day long. So you have two people going at each other just trying to get through the day.

It takes a special inner strength to channel that frustration. Isaiah 41:10 says, "Fear not, for I am with you; Be not dismayed for I am your God. I will strengthen you. Yes, I will help you, I will hold you with My righteous right hand." God is the source of strength to deal with this frustration. Frustration is inevitable when you are a caregiver. Just find the strength to persevere and overcome it. And remember that you are probably not alone in your frustration.

Chapter

18

Rest Assured

I thought I had experienced tiredness to the point of exhaustion before. But I did not know what true fatigue was until this time in my life. I had my own house to keep clean, laundry to wash, garden and yard to tend, and other chores. Fortunately, I have a wonderful husband who helped me. But I also helped my dad perform all these same chores at his house while caring for my mom. That, in and of itself, can be very tiring. All the emotional and physical stress, however, makes it difficult to sleep. You feel so tired that sleep should not be an issue. But you lay there, tossing and turning, because sleep eludes you. I would try all types of natural and homeopathic remedies. Sometimes they worked, and sometimes they didn't. When the simple non-pharmacologic tricks didn't work, I saw my doctor about it. He prescribed medication for occasional use. Getting my sleep and rest was crucial to my ability to effectively care for my mom.

There were several occasions when we thought my mom was going to die. Dad and I would sit up day and night to attend to her during these events. But she had such a strong will to live. There was also the fact that she would not let go until God's appointed time. Those twenty-four-hour vigils took so much out of me. I truly could not rest. My mind would not shut down long enough for me to sleep. I was afraid if I slept, something would happen to her that maybe I could have prevented. I felt I had some control over her life or death, which was not the case at all. I was not allowing myself to rest in the Lord. That is when I had to accept the promise of Psalm 4:8: "I will both lie down in peace and sleep; for You alone, O Lord, make me dwell in safety."

I should've feared nothing. I should've slept and rested peacefully, knowing that God was in control. He knows already what is in our future. He knows the precise second we will breathe our last breath on earth and take our first in heaven. So fully trusting in God will allow you to truly rest.

Chapter

19

A Worry Wart

My parents used to call me a worry wart when I was younger. I would worry about making good grades. I worried about having friends. I worried about making the team for whatever sport was in season. I worried about getting into college. The list could go on. I did stop short of worrying about something to worry about though.

As a caregiver, I worried about the condition of my mom. Was I doing a good job caring for her? Did I understand what she was trying to communicate to me accurately? What if I did the wrong thing? I also worried about my dad. Did he fully comprehend what was going on with Mom? His health was not the best, so I worried about how he was doing physically.

Jan Blakely

I worried about how he was going to cope when my mom passed on. I worried about what I was going to do when they were both gone.

Even when hospice became involved with my mom's care, I still worried. Were we doing enough to make her last days comfortable? What could I do to add quality to her last days? I was robbing myself of life by worrying. First Peter 5:7 says, "Casting all your care upon Him, for He cares for you." I needed to hand off my worries to the one who holds our life in His hands. If He can speak the universe into existence, then He can take care of anything and everything I could ever worry about.

Worrying has never accomplished anything. I needed to take lessons from my younger brother. He just let everything roll off him like water off a duck's back. His attitude came across as if he did not care. But what was really going on was that he was laying the worry down at the Savior's feet and was not carrying the burden himself. So lay the worries down, and, in the words of St. Augustine, "Let go and let God."

Chapter
20

An Emotion Understood

Since my mom was diagnosed with dementia, I have cried enough tears to water my garden for a season. Sometimes the tears were precipitated by a change in Mom's condition, a bad day, or an event such as a holiday. Days that should have been full of joy were filled with tears. Sometimes the tears came for no reason at all other than needing to have a good cry. It can be so cathartic sometimes to sit down and have a good cry. There were times my husband would walk in and find me crying. He would ask if I was okay and ask why I was upset. All I could say was "just because." Sometimes you may not know the reason behind the tears. When close friends asked about Mom, tears would start to well up in my eyes as I tried to update them.

Many times I would ask God why. Why did my mom have to get dementia? Why did our lives have to be turned upside down? Why was I being robbed of my mom at this time in our lives? God is okay with us asking why as long as it is in the right spirit of the heart.

I was not the only one who shed tears. There were days when Mom had moments of clarity and shed her own share of tears. She knew what her condition was and even recognized her own decline. As she approached the last weeks of her life, she would cry while trying to let us know how much she loved us. Of course, then the tears would be reciprocated by my dad and me.

Jesus experienced the same emotions while He was here on earth. John 11:35 tells us that "Jesus wept." He felt grief and heartache, just as we do. So He fully understands our emotions and knows about every tear we shed. So cry those tears, and know that you are in good company.

Chapter
21

Just a Wanderer

One of the biggest fears for the family of someone with dementia is that the person will wander off and get lost or hurt. My mom wandered away from home on several occasions, but we were fortunate enough to find her unharmed. My parents lived in a rural community. We used to be able to go outside and work in the yard or garden without fear of Mom wandering off. But that changed.

While we were working on a new cattle stable, I periodically went in the house to check on Mom. One day, however, she was nowhere to be found. We searched the entire property. We called neighbors and enlisted their help. We got in the car and drove to the nearest businesses that were about one-half mile from our house. No one had seen her. My dad and I met back at his house. We decided to notify the police, as we had been looking for her for about forty five minutes without success. As I reached for the phone, it rang. It was a neighbor calling. She had found Mom walking on the road coming back toward home. Mom had decided to go to the mailbox to get the mail. But she got turned around and went the wrong way.

I have no idea how far she went or even what made her turn around and come back. I can only believe that she had angels watching over and guiding her. Isaiah 30:21 says, "Your ears shall hear a word behind you, saying, 'This is the way, walk in it,' whenever you turn to the right hand or whenever you turn to the left." So I truly believe that God was with her, helping to lead her back home.

I am not naive enough to think that we did not need to take precautions to prevent this from happening again. I realize how lucky we were that she was found unhurt. We installed door alarms on all the doors, and we never left her alone again. We made adjustments in our routines so that someone was always inside with her. On beautiful days we took her out with us and let her sit in a chair to watch over us while we did our chores.

It is important to put safeguards in place early on to monitor the goings and comings of your loved one. Not every family has the outcome that our family had. You do not want to be one of the other statistics.

Chapter
22

Have an Outlet

My son called me as he was driving home from work on a Friday afternoon. First he inquired as to how my mom was doing. She had been declining in health rapidly over the past couple of weeks. Then he told me he was on his way to the local high school track so he could run. I thought it odd that he would not be heading straight home from work on a Friday. He shared with me that he needed to work out some stress. I asked what he had to be stressed about. Then he started to describe his litany of stressors. Mom (his grandmother) was at the top of the list.

I had been so wrapped up in my own stress that I had not been able to see how my mom's condition impacted others. My children may not have been directly involved with her care, but they did what they could to help. That aside, they loved their grandmother and were very concerned for her well-being. They also loved me and cared about the impact that this situation had on me. They saw how stressed I was.

My brother lives several hours away and was not able to be as involved in Mom's care. But he came when he could to give me a break and felt stress about not being able to help more. My husband was affected because he had to watch me go down this road, so he was definitely impacted by it. Then there was my dad. The toll this ordeal was taking on him was clearly visible on his face. During one of our Memory Care visits, he participated in a survey for caregivers. It asked him to rate the level of stress he felt, being a caregiver. He rated it as extreme. I was surprised that he openly shared such information.

It was an eye opening revelation. It is extremely stressful being the caregiver of someone with dementia. It is even more revealing when you realize that the stress is not limited to you. Every single family member feels it in a very different way. Like my son going to run as his outlet, you have to have a positive way to release the stress. I love physical work. Being able to work in the yard or garden is a good outlet for me. But it also helps to look to the source of peace to provide relief from stress. God tells us, "You will keep him in perfect peace, whose mind is stayed on You because he trusts in You" (Isaiah 26:3). Stress is part of life. But don't let it steal your focus or your joy. Learn to manage it instead of allowing it to manage you.

Chapter
23

Randy, Jan, and Ronny

If you have siblings, you may recall a time when you were younger, and your parents would call out names on a list until they came to the right name of the child they wanted. Even as a parent I have found myself calling out the names of all my kids until I got to the name of the child I was addressing. Every experience through your life is registered in your brain. Your brain gets so full of stuff as you get older. I think sometimes all that knowledge just bumps around in your head and gets all muddled. At least that excuse sounds good.

Confusion is one of the clinical signs of dementia. It might start off in a subtle way, just like getting names mixed up. But the confusion progresses and becomes more pronounced. At that point, it is sometimes noticed and hopefully diagnosed.

I remember that when my mom's dementia was still in the early phase, she would get ingredients mixed up while cooking. One time she put vinegar in the mashed potatoes instead of milk. Before Mom's confusion got so bad that it was unsafe for her to drive, she would be driving somewhere and become confused about where she was going or how to get there. She eventually started asking my kids to drive her. Fortunately for everyone, she stopped driving on her own volition. Her confusion might be exhibited when she put on two different shoes when getting dressed. Then it progressed to the point of not being able to recognize her loved ones.

A lot of times people blame God when bad things happen. If God is so good, then why did He let this happen? There is an order in life. Unfortunately, that order also includes illness and death. Confusion seems to be contradictory to order. First Corinthians 14:33 addresses harmony of the church by saying, "For God is not the author of confusion, but of peace." However, I think it is fitting to apply it to my mom. God did not give her over to the confusion. It was just a symptom of her disease. But He could be our source of peace as we dealt with her confusion and her illness.

Chapter
24

Be an Encourager

Sometimes, as a caregiver, it is easy to get all wrapped up in how your life is being affected. You give up a job. You sacrifice time with a spouse. You lose your identity as a person because it is all about taking care of someone else. You can't sleep. You can't eat, or maybe you overeat. There is no time for exercise or even cleaning your own house. Woe is me; poor pitiful me. But wait a minute! You still have all your faculties, and they are functioning normally. But the person you are taking care of does not.

If you just insert your loved one's name in place of your own on that self-pity list, you will see he or she needs encouragement as much as you do, if not more so. Your loved one can no longer work a job, have quality time with someone else, or go out and do things independently. He or she has lost a sense of self to a high degree and is vulnerable and prey to self-serving people. You are able to get away from it even if briefly. You can at least carry on an intelligent conversation with another person. Your loved one cannot find a source of escape, much less carry on an intelligent conversation.

You can find sources of encouragement. But your loved one can't. So even though it may seem to be one more thing on your list to do for your loved one, find it in yourself to give him or her encouragement. This in turn will be an encouragement for you. Romans 12:8 says, "He who exhorts, in exhortation; he who gives, with liberality; he who leads, with diligence; he who shows mercy, with cheerfulness."

Being an encourager is a gift. Like other gifts, when given away there is as much joy for the giver as for the recipient. So the encouragement you give to your loved one will come back to you. There is nothing sweeter than the smile of your loved one that is there just for you.

Chapter
25

Tugging at the Heart Strings

I had to go out of town for a few days to be with my husband's family. My mother-in-law is suffering from a type of dementia as well. It is like a mirror image of my own mother. My father-in-law is the primary caregiver, just like my dad. My husband and I joke about what is in store for us in our golden years. Which one of us will be affected, and which one will be the caregiver? But if we both get it, neither one of us will know or care. Our poor kids!

Anyway, I had some apprehension about being away. My brother came to stay to help my dad care for my mom. Of course, I thought no one could do as good a job as I did. But that was in my own mind. I left detailed instructions about her medication schedule and her daily routines. Keeping those afflicted with dementia in their familiar routines helps to keep them stable and calm.

I called daily to check on her. Okay, I admit it was a couple of times a day. I wasn't sure if my mom even comprehended that I was gone. But during one of our phone conversations, she asked me if she was ever going to see me again. That really pulled at my heart strings. I knew she was being well cared for. But a mother and daughter have a special bond. And that bond takes on a whole new dimension when one of the two becomes the caregiver for the other. The focus is making sure that he or she is cared for and that every need is met with all the love and compassion imaginable.

There is a prayer from Genesis 31:49 that I quoted from the Bible as I left my mom for my trip: "May the Lord watch between you and me when we are absent one from another." I know God was watching over my mom while I was gone. I had to trust in His provision for her. Through that trust I was able to relax and enjoy the time with my extended family.

Chapter

26

It's All about Family

Starting from when my children were young until they left home, my mom was very involved in their lives. Since I had to work, she was my source of childcare between their infant to toddler years. She made all occasions special for them. She was at all their events: sports, drama, music, award ceremonies, and graduations. For her it was not about spending money on the grandkids. It was about spending time—quality time. She would incorporate learning into their play. She started teaching them a basic foundation of education. She taught them about God and His love for us. She taught them principles of moral living. She taught them not only by word but by being a living example.

She was a wonderful mother and grandmother. She was the example of what you think a grandmother should be. I believe if you look up the word *grandmother* in the dictionary, you will see a picture of my mom.

My kids were aware of Mom's onset of dementia as it began in their mid- to late teens. They would joke about it. I believe that resorting to humor was their way of coping. When they left for college, they would check in on her via phone calls or visits when they were home. But as they were establishing their own lives, they did not shower her with the attention that I felt she deserved. I know it wasn't easy for them to come see her, since they either lived out of town or had families of their own that needed their attention. But as she declined and grew closer to dying, I wished that they had put forth more effort to see or talk to her. It would've only taken a few minutes, since her capacity for conversation was very small. She was always so happy when they came to visit. I guess though that it was hard for them to see her in that state. They preferred to remember her when was vivacious and active in their lives.

She was the epitome of a strong woman. I only hope to be a fraction of the woman, wife, mother, and grandmother that she was. "Children's children are the crown of old men and the glory of children is their father" (Proverbs 17:6). This verse says it all so perfectly. I am one proud daughter of my fabulous mother.

Chapter
27

A Special Occasion

Holidays can be difficult when someone in your family has dementia. You go through the motions, wanting to make this one the best ever because it might be the last. Holidays can really exhaust you physically and emotionally to the point of almost not being able to enjoy them. I took my mom to a mother and daughter tea. Mom enjoyed it to the extent she was capable of enjoying such an event. I did it primarily for a selfish reason. I wanted to make a special memory for myself. At Thanksgiving I cooked all of Mom's favorite foods. I wanted it to be most enjoyable for her.

Christmas was very hard. What kind of gift do you give someone who has dementia? A few seconds after opening it, she would forget it. You didn't really want to give something expensive because there was a high probability of it getting lost and/or misplaced because she wanted to put it somewhere safe. So you ended up giving a few basic necessity gifts: socks, pajamas, and so forth.

Christmas was always Mom's favorite holiday. I would put forth a lot of effort to decorate so that she could enjoy it. Then she would ask every day if it was time to take everything down. There were days when the ornaments would be removed from the tree because she thought Christmas was over. The big conundrum was whether or not to take pictures. On the one hand, you wanted pictures of the holiday, especially when it was one of few times a year that everyone came together. There was also the thought that it could be the last holiday with her. On the other hand, you didn't want pictures of her in her current state of illness. You wanted to remember her when she was at her peak in life.

As the disease progressed and death drew near, holidays almost became a burden. It was easier to just look at them as ordinary days on the calendar. Thankfully she made it to her birthday. She appreciated all the fuss. Next came Easter, which gives us hope of life in heaven when this earthly life comes to an end. I dreaded the holidays to come when she would no longer be with me. Psalm 43:5 says, "Why are you cast down, O my soul? And why are you disquieted within me? Hope in God; For I shall yet praise Him, the help of my countenance and my God." I will just have to find a way to celebrate her and the holidays in her absence. I guess new traditions will have to be created just to get through the holidays. But for now I will continue to cherish each one that she made it to and not worry about what the future holds.

Chapter
28

A Glorious Reunion

I returned home after being gone for four days. After unpacking the car, I went straight to Mom's house to check on her. I knew that she had been well cared for while I was gone. I had checked in on her at least once—sometimes more often—each day. While driving home, my brother called and gave me a detailed accounting of how Mom had fared in my absence. He said he felt that she was more aware of what was going on than she was able to convey or that we gave her credit for.

So when I walked in and called her name, she turned to look at me, and her whole countenance lit up. She really was glad to see me. I asked her if she missed me, and I got the typically limited response of yeah. Of course it made me feel special. I joked with her about my dad and brother not knowing how she and I did things and that I had returned to rescue her. She kept patting my face and rubbing my hand. That was her way of letting me know she was aware that I had been gone, and she was happy that I had returned. Of course she had enjoyed the time that my brother had spent with her. But being a primary caregiver, along with my dad, we had a special bond. So it was a very heartwarming reunion. As good as this reunion was it will be nothing compared to the one in heaven. "Then we who are alive and remain shall be caught up together with them in the clouds to meet the Lord in the air. And thus we shall always be with the Lord" (1 Thessalonians 4:17).

Mom was fully restored when she entered heaven where there is no more sickness and no more dementia. I just look forward to the day when I can join her in heaven, and I can see her in her glorified state.

Chapter

29

Don't Give Up

There used to be a time when family members cared for each other at home. There were limited alternatives for care of a loved one. But in the past, it was more likely that family members tended to settle locally when starting their own families. Today we live in a society on the move. It is far more common for offspring to set up shop hundreds of miles away in another state or even another country. So who is left to care for parents when they get to the point where they can no longer care for themselves?

There are now various levels of healthcare facilities to care for loved ones, including those with dementia. It could be a senior community, assisted living center, skilled nursing facility, or even a locked Alzheimer's unit.

But you can still choose to keep them at home and have a non-licensed care provider come to the home to help. There are always ads for people looking for a live-in caregiver or someone looking to fill that type of position. But you also have the option to care for your loved one yourself. That is the option we chose for my mom.

My dad made a promise to my mom many years ago that, as long as he was alive and able, he would take care of her and never put her in a nursing home. I did what I could to help my dad honor that promise. It was not easy. Some days I think how much easier on me it would have been and how I could have had my life back if she had been in a nursing home instead of at home. But then I realized that I was being selfish. For eighteen years my mom's focus was caring for me. It was the least that I could do—give her a few years back in return. It was no easy task though. Some days it was the hardest thing I have ever done. The Bible says, "And let us not grow weary while doing good, for in due season we shall reap if we do not lose heart" (Galatians 6:9).

Caring for a loved one at home is not the right decision for everyone, but it was the right decision for my family. But if you go that route, hang in there and don't give up. The reward is in knowing in your heart that you have done the right thing for your loved one.

Chapter
30

Moral of the Story

My mom loved the written word. She was an avid reader. Our house looked like a branch library because there were so many books. She loved to write stories, but poetry was her forte. She had several poems published. She continued to write some poems and stories even after the onset of dementia. There was, however, a discernible change in the writing style and grammar after the dementia set in. She wrote a poem for her physician and staff at Memory Care. She used to keep her collected writings in a notebook. But as dementia set in, we weren't able to find the whole collection. We have found several pieces tucked away here and there. That is one frustrating facet of dementia. The person will put something away for safekeeping, but it tends to be lost forever.

She loved to keep journals or spiral notebooks lying around everywhere so she could quickly write something down when she had an idea or needed to make a note. One day, while looking through some of the notebooks, I found the following story she had written titled *The Fly.*

> There was a fly in the kitchen. There were never any crumbs for him to eat. He was getting very hungry. One day the housekeeper was very busy. She left a piece of bologna on the table. The little fly ate it. He got so full of food he crawled over and went up the broom handle. Then he fell on his face.
>
> The moral to the story is: Don't fly off the handle if you are full of baloney.

This story goes right along with Proverbs 14:33, which says, "Wisdom rests in the heart of him who has understanding, but what is in the heart of fools is made known." When we thought that she did not have a clue as to what was going on, she put us in our place with her story. Do not assume that your loved one does not have a clue. He or she might understand more than you realize.

Thanks, Mom, for the words of wisdom.

Chapter
31

Starts with a Smile

Mom always had a smile to share with others. She would tell them how pretty they looked or make some remark that would put a smile on their faces. She had a way of making every person feel special. She would try to make someone laugh by telling a story. But usually the story made no sense, was hard to follow, or was full of made-up words and content. Just the ridiculousness of it would get you tickled, and the laughter would start from there. But sometimes you would laugh to keep from crying because of the heartache you felt as you watched your loved one struggle to fit in. It was heart-wrenching to see what the dementia was doing to my mom. It was robbing her of her ability to effectively communicate. But it never robbed her of her smile.

As death approached and even after she passed away, family and friends gathered. We shared stories about Mom. From the need to overcome the grief, we typically shared stories that brought joy and laughter. It did our hearts good to hear others tell stories of what she had done to bring joy and happiness to their lives.

Proverbs 14:13 says, "Even in laughter the heart may sorrow, and the end of mirth may be grief." The jocularity of people coming together to enjoy companionship and acknowledge the life of someone who has passed was rooted in sorrow. But out of that sorrow I can reflect back on the stories shared, and they bring a smile back to my face. So the smiles that Mom started have gone full circle.

Share your stories about your loved one now, and enjoy the time of laughter.

Chapter
32

Love What You Do

What can be more fun than to love what you do? This is a rhetorical question. But if you love what you do, then you will find joy in doing it. How much more joy and fun can there be than when you are caring for your loved one with dementia? Yeah, right.

It is so easy to say and so hard to live it out when you are caring for loved ones with dementia. How can it be fun to care for those who might see you as a stranger and refuse to do what you are asking of them? Where is the fun when they are incontinent while you are trying to have a meal? Where is the fun when they take scissors and cut up their clothes or cut off their own hair? Where is the fun when they slip away from you in a crowd and you panic in search of them?

Jan Blakely

But there is love as you care for all their needs while reminding them of your relationship. There is love as you gently and meticulously clean them and return them to their meals. There is love as you find alternate clothes to wear or rework their hairstyles. There is love when you are reunited after they wander off, and the panic subsides.

Psalm 128:2 says, "When you eat the labor of your hands, you shall be happy, and it shall be well with you." You do everything you do because of love. There might not always be fun in every day of life with a dementia patient. But if you do what you do because of love, then you will find the fun. If you cannot love what you do, then you will never be satisfied.

Chapter
33

Mission Impossible

God does not always use the best and brightest to accomplish what He wants done. He uses the right person and the right circumstance. Caring for someone with dementia is physically, mentally, emotionally, and spiritually taxing. You have to stay on your toes all the time—literally around the clock. As your loved one declines, you question your ability to continue on as a caregiver.

One time my mom was physically having a bad day. We were walking through the house together when she collapsed. The nurse in me kicked in gear and wanted to initiate the process of assessment and intervention. But the daughter in me—who understood the outcome we could be facing—wanted to let things go their natural course. It truly was an internal struggle. Fortunately, she responded quickly, and no intervention was required.

I relayed the scenario to a prayer partner and added that I was not sure I could handle following through with our DNR (do not resuscitate) decision when the time came. She promptly reminded me that I could. She reminded me, with God's power and direction, I could do exactly what He had put me here to do.

Mark 10:27 says, "With men, it is impossible, but not with God; for with God all things are possible." You may not think you are capable of providing the care required for your loved one. But remember: the Bible is full of examples where God used the insignificant to accomplish what seemed to be impossible. If He did it for them, He can also equip you to do it.

Chapter

34

Calm in the Storm

When dementia takes hold of someone's brain, it changes that person. Sometimes it can turn your little darling into an unrecognizable monster. You are afraid to be in public with your monster for fear of what he or she might say or do. Language that might have been taboo in a normal state might now be commonplace. Words said may be harsh, demeaning, or vulgar. Jokes, stories, or songs may take on a sexual connotation. This type of thing can be very embarrassing because it always happens when you least expect it.

The bad behavior is not limited to vocabulary. Your loved one may engage in questionable activities. You go to a store, and when you walk out, your loved one has in his or her possession an item that you know was not paid for. You go to a restaurant together. Food gets thrown on the floor. Your loved one may walk by and pick up the tip money that was left for the waitress or walk up to total strangers and give them unexpected hugs.

My mom's doctor tried to prepare us for this. As a result, we carried little business cards with us that we could hand out to the unsuspecting victims. The card explained that the person with us suffered from dementia and to please excuse any offensive behavior. You never can predict how others will react to the behavior of your loved one. It is like living in a constant storm, never knowing when the next lightning strike or clap of thunder will occur. So you live life constantly on edge.

Philippians 4:7 tells us, "And the peace of God, which surpasses all understanding, will guard your hearts and minds through Christ Jesus." The Lord will take care of the storms you encounter as you care for your loved one. He will either calm the storm or calm you. Either way, He gets you through.

Chapter

35

Job Well Done

By our very nature we like to hear praise. It starts in our youth. Children are driven by praise. The more you praise them, the more they want to do for you. This desire carries on through adult life. A spouse loves to hear a partner praise him or her for what has been accomplished—a clean house, a wonderful meal, and so forth. An employee appreciates praise from the boss during the periodic performance review process. People enter competitions at local fairs, sporting events, or challenges so that they can win a prize and receive the praise that goes with it. I enjoy sewing. I love to show people what I have made in order to show off my accomplishment and receive praise for it.

When you are a caregiver for a family member with dementia, you are not going to be showered with accolades of praise. You are doing well if your loved one still knows who you are. As a follower of Christ, the parable of the faithful servant is one that we associate with receiving our praise from God when we enter heaven. We long to hear "Well done, good and faithful servant; you were faithful over a few things, I will make you ruler over many things. Enter into the joy of your Lord" (Matthew 25:21).

My mom had dementia for several years. Fortunately, it was caught early, and the decline initially was slow. But there was an exponential decline in her cognitively and physically in the last few months of her life. During one of the acute illnesses, as my mom was lying in bed and I was sitting at her side, she had a very brief moment of clarity. She put her hand on my face and clearly said, with love in her eyes, "Thank you, honey. You've done a good job." All the anguish, heartache, stress, and loss of sleep were worth it to hear that simple phrase come from the lips and heart of that precious woman. Thank you, Mom! That was the best praise I could ever hear this side of heaven.

Chapter
36

Life Eternal

When your loved one is diagnosed with dementia, it is like being given a death sentence. He or she is robbed of life while still alive because of the impact on the brain. Physical death is a blessing when it comes.

My mom was a follower of Christ. She never hesitated to share her testimony with others. I fully believe that there will be so many more souls in heaven because of my mom. Because of her faith, she knew that when she died a physical death she would be given life everlasting in heaven with a glorified body.

The incidence of dementia is increasing. So too is death associated with dementia. So much research is being done to find the cause and cure for dementia. But we are not there yet. My mom lived with dementia for at least eleven years, or at least it was eleven years from the time of diagnosis. As her mind wore out, so did her precious little body. There were days when she was clear in thought; she would then pray for death to come without further delay. She did not want to be a burden to her family who loved her. But she also made the best of every day she was given. She knew that my dad and I loved her. She understood that caring for her was an act of love for us. She was never a burden. Mom fully understood Philippians 1:21, which says, "For to me, to live is Christ and to die is gain." She knew that as long as she had breath, she was a living testimony to Christ. But she also knew she would gain the ultimate reward when the time came for her to pass from this life.

Mom is gone from us now. As she looks down from heaven, I hope she fully understands and appreciates that it was my honor to care for her. I do not have any regrets, and I would do it all over again. Thank you, Mom, for all that you did for me. Thank you for allowing me to care for you. I look forward to seeing you again one day in heaven. I love you, Mom.